Langu

# Language You Refuse to Learn

## Poems

## Claudia M. Stanek

Bright Hill Press

Treadwell, NY
2014

# Language You Refuse to Learn
## Poems
### Claudia M. Stanek

At Hand Poetry Chapbook Series, No. 39
Book & Cover Design: Bertha Rogers
Editor in Chief: Bertha Rogers
Editorial Assistant: Lawrence E. Shaw
Editorial Intern: Kyrra Howard

ISBN: 978-1892471772

Library of Congress Control Number: 2014948299

NYSCA
New York State Council on the Arts

[clmp]

*Language You Refuse to Learn* is published by Bright Hill
Press, Inc., a not-for-profit 501 (c) (3) literary and educa-
tional organization founded in 1992. The organization is
registered with the New York State Department of State,
Office of Charities Registration. Publication of *Language
You Refuse to Learn* is made possible, in part, with public
funds from the Literature Program of the New York
State Council on the Arts, a State Agency, and supported
by Governor Andrew Cuomo and the New York State
Legislature.

Editorial Address: Bright Hill Press, Inc., 94 Church
Street, Treadwell, NY 13846-4607; Voice: 607-829-
5055; Fax: 607-829-5054; Website: www.brighthillpress.
org; Email:wordthur@stny.rr.com

# Acknowledgements

Grateful acknowledgement is made below to the publications, in print or online, where these poems were originally published, sometimes with different titles or in slightly different versions.

"Alive": *Animus*
"Stakes": *Briar Cliff Review*
"Hide": *The Chaffin Journal*
"Left Behind": *Eleventh Muse*
"Appendage": *Main Channel Voices*
"A Walking Tour of Central Europe on American Soil":
    *Redactions: Poetry & Poetics*
"Shock Treatment": *Summer Songs: An Anthology from
    the Third Annual Gell Center Summer Poetry Festival, 2004*
"That Year": *Red Wheelbarrow*
"More Than White": *The Woman in the Mirror:
    An Anthology of Women Celebrating Women*
"Late Afternoon, February 16, 1905": *Whistling Shade*

# Contents

*Words are insufficient to thank all the poets, family, and friends—far too many to name—whose patience, creativity, and support made the completion of this chapbook possible. Bardzo dziękuję.*

*—For Polonia*

## *Late Afternoon, February 16, 1905*

A chorus of gulls calls
the *Barbarossa* into the harbor.
You are just one kerchiefed girl
next to innumerable others,
some with heads uncovered, most
whose husbands bar their view.
You shield your son's fright
within the fabric of your worn
wool skirt. A tattered wrap,
one satchel all you bring, owning
little to leave in Polish fields
sown for Austrian overlords.
Your husband, gone before you,
has prepared a place for you,
the boy and the daughter offered
to the ocean three days ago,
the stench of her loss now overcome
by the smell of unknown chemicals
that punctuate your arrival.

As you watch the green sea
brown, factories reach their smoke

for you, pulling the ship to the shore
and its dense forest of brick and mortar.
You uncover your son and his fear, lift
him up on your hip. You both squint
at your new sovereign, her torch
thrusting upward above alien
shadows, wonder what is
written in the book she holds.

Diverse tongues converge
in heated relief as peoples swell
onto unknown ground, you and they
sick of each other's rank continental
bodies, freight to be hurriedly unloaded
so New Country goods can fill
the ship's hold. The swell shoves you
and your son in a surge of hunger
for the land you expect to till. *Your land*
though you do not yet know
what else must be left behind to find it.

After hours spent waiting, at last
you hear repeated over and over
the first words of the language
you will refuse to learn. Here,
you set down the boy who clings less
tightly now. You hand papers to a foreigner
separated from you both by a half-wall
and bars. He reads the symbols written
on the page in German, not even your own
language, though you could not have read it
even if it were. You do not know what
this ink will mean. This man looks down
at you—you are so short—and your boy,
speaks to you as his eyes examine
the gray of yours. You do not respond.
Your son shrugs off his fear, removes his cap
and, tapping the counter to draw
the man's attention, mouths
strange sounds he would speak for you
for the next seventy years.

## The Lesson

The babushka knew country rats could learn as much as children, how repeated effort without correction bolstered vermin courage. Each time the feed shed's door hinge squeaked, they scattered at her armed chase. She thought to bait a box trap their instinct could not resist. She stoked the wood stove, brought her grandson from his studies to observe. A poker flamed, glowed past red to white. With gloved hands she retrieved one of the thieves, burned out each eye, and released it. The boy swallowed his tears when she slapped his cheek with her ungloved hand as the fire cooled.

*Surname*
  *przystanek (Polish): stop, way station*

A Czech tells me it is common.
In Polish it means nothing
without a prefix. A German

tells my black-haired sister
it is not Polish but Austrian,
which she believes. She disregards

the history of the central Europe
Dad's family escaped—the era
of Poland sliced like elderberry pie

then eaten by gluttonous Hapsburgs.
Perhaps my sister is the Nazi
our babci purported such girls to be,

as she did our mother whose hair
was even blacker, eyebrows too,
in their precisely sharpened arches.

I darkened my hair as a teen since
I could not color my blue eyes brown.
Nor could I sing the high 'C' in hymns

with them and was left to sit
in audiences with captive senior
citizens; most could not hear

the harmony. The German-American
mother-daughter duo sang, chins lifted
in unison, faces pointing to heaven.

My chin pulled my head to my chest
like those asleep beside me,
until the requisite applause.

*Locomotive*

It is cloudless blue sky mid-July, the only month snow never dares curse this northern air. Siblings more than a decade apart in age, my sister and I walk the line that determines the good from the bad. She assures me: *No trains will come.* But the tracks groan and quiver.

Fear is my stoic foot stuck in its sneaker between wood and steel. Fear is the lack of strength in the grip of my sister's soft hands. I rip my foot from its bound ties as the horn squalls, free from those same railroad tracks where thirty years earlier a spring dose of lake effect snow and a dozing signalman conspired to splatter Grandfather's body into a random palette of flesh on drifts of white.

Middle-aged, I always stop at railroad crossings as if driving a cautionary yellow busload of kids. My restive eye searches for that engine numbered for me. The grandfather I never knew waits to take my ticket.

## A Walking Tour of Central Europe
### on American Soil

Gravel surrenders to warm macadam
as you near Depew where the Poles live.
Blisters on your big toes, you carry
the offending shoes, walk
barefoot. Your calloused soles
don't mind the move from stones
to pavement, not after
all those summers spent shoeless.
To your right is Dumbrowski's
Bait & Tackle where Dad bought line
and sinkers to last the summer, ammo
for deer season. On the way to the foundry
where he spent thirty years
snuffling in silicate dust,
is the D & L Bakery—as if
Lancaster's Germans would buy their kuchen
there, no matter how sweet the smell.
Your mother did, but she'd lived
on the border most of her life. Just before
the train tracks, the carillon chimes
at St. Augie's where mass is still
said in Polish.

Another block down is the house
of the hairdresser who blackened
your mother's roots every three weeks.
You would sit in one of those dryer-chairs
and read magazines filled with fictions
you didn't understand—
like the housewife who danced bare-breasted.
Across the street is the Village Inn
where your dad used to shoot craps on pay day,
finally off limits now.
If he were lucky or felt guilty, he'd bring home
beef on kimmelweck for Mother.
At Gould Ave. you'd have to choose:
walk west two blocks to the factory's gate
or head east toward Lancaster
where you mother went to the Lutheran Church,
and took her dry cleaning.
Maybe you'd stop at Deutchlander's
for an ice cream in a sugar cone.
But you'd have to put your shoes back on
to be served, even being half-German.

## The Price of Heaven

For thirty-four dollars today, I can waterproof my eyelashes before heading out to the beach on the Great Lake. I could buy a nice silk scarf, a few cotton tees, or a decent pair of sandals on clearance.

~

In 1905 with thirty-four dollars strapped around her waist, Babci took her son and daughter, left the migrant-worker life, got on a boat, and lived in steerage with livestock, next to the dung pile, from Galicy to Dresden to western New York, where her husband had already settled three years earlier. Once there, Babci only traveled as far as she could walk in a day while her husband wandered.

~

In 1970 my father would buy Babci new calico kerchiefs, men's plaid flannel shirts, and lace-up work boots she'd wear until they wore through, all for thirty-four dollars at K-Mart.

~

In 1942 she could have paid thirty-four dollars for the priest to say enough masses to rescue her husband's soul, once she learned he died somewhere near Chicago. She never wore mascara, so it didn't run when she didn't cry.

## More Than White

### In memory of Evelyn Stanek

No tinge of blue like the hair
of so many at that age,
yours still more than white
and you hadn't even seen seventy
before breath forgot your name.
That wig you sported
in the gaunt days of chemo
hinted at blue, more
than the silvered glass
reflecting the present
every morning,
every night,
as you looked into death's face,
less than the white of the life
you wished you'd owned.

Your hair grew back,
more than white
with the slightest suggestion
of that natural curl
you'd always claimed,

---

finally yours for free,
courtesy of your HMO.
But you never got out of bed
to flip the lie into truth.
Even as your body lay
cushioned upon white satin,
the blue of your mother's suit
that you chose to wear forever
echoed in the wig
strangers decided was
more the real you.

## Stakes

Kneeling as if in prayer at the Lutheran Church
on Sunday morning, Dad prepares
to give his Big Boy tomato plants
backbones against the expected weight
of their fruit. He savors the menthol cigarette
stuck to his lower lip as he unsnakes twine
taken from his shirt pocket.

Ash falls into soil. He returns smoke to the air,
weaves twine around each vine and its stake.
I walk barefoot through the dry dirt
to his side, eyes at his level.
*Why do they need to stand up so straight?*

He bends the end of one toward me, singles out
the small bubble of green beginning to grow.
*If tomatoes lie on the ground, they will rot*
*and be no damn good to eat.*
He puts the unused twine back
in his pocket, smacks the last cigarette
from its pack, lights the end, and extracts
all the dead butts from the ground.

---

*Dew*


In an August evening, Mother plants me
where gravel embraces pavement.
Most neighbors are nestled
in their naugahyde recliners, watching
black and white dramas unfold in two
dimensions. Dusk's invaders attack
my legs and arms through Mother Goose
pajamas. Their hunger pinks my skin
with bumps I do not yet know
how to count. My head, still wet,
aches under bedtime curlers
wound too tight. I shake.
Mother waits, expecting the lines
of my debut. She bends to my height,
directs me to cup my hands and call
toward the house two doors down.
Dew begins to coat weeds long in need
of mowing. *Papa*—my voice, too soft.
Night settles too fast.
Barefoot, my toes grab stones
as I follow her to the bottom
of the driveway's "U" and into our house

where I lie in the too-big-for-me bed,
where sleep is only a dream
until the screen door bangs shut.

*Left Behind*

Because the key fit and the lock turned, she opened
the door just enough to see a light
had been left on, then pulled
the door closed again.

Because a light had been left on, she grabbed
the knob as if gripping a steering wheel
in a blizzard, gave it a hard turn before
reluctance drove her away.

Because reluctance wanted to master her, she opened
the door and entered the kitchen, its mildew
greeting and scattered mouse droppings
her only invitation to come in.

Because mildew and feces are unseemly,
she scouted for bare spots on the tile
and tip-toed to the countertop
licked clean of crumbs.

Because cleanliness marked her home
and not this, her mother's, she found
a pail and long-dried sponge
to begin the necessary work.

Because her work required water and someone
had shut it off, she looked out the picture
window above the sink at the bare birch
she would have to leave behind.

Because she had been left behind, she left empty
pail and sponge, flicked off the light switch,
closed the door behind her and left
the key with the clutter.

## Shock Treatment

Round and round he counts
the corners of the room, floor to ceiling,
ceiling to floor—their number changing
each time. A glint
in the silvered light above
pricks his eye, his own
contorted visage staring him down.
Electrodes suck his skin.
Memory reaches for that dead end
street where the willow was—
the one he planted the day he finished
the house—a swampy pond
in its place. His arms strapped down
like logs on a flatbed
going to a mill, he enters
the abandoned house. Whiteness blares.
He cannot close his ears
or cover his eyes. It is 1964 but
he must climb rotting stairs to 1979.
He is unable to grasp
the rail, his bare feet uncertain.

His scream is muted
to spare his tongue. On broken glass,
he drags thoughts up and up.
To the right, a water-stained door,
to the left, another; neither
made by him. Warped,
the one he chooses sticks,
but with one hard shove,
jolts open.

## Not Answering

The telephone chime pleads
and pleads for an answer.
Mother's made sure to push
the princess phone to the back
of the kitchen counter
just out of reach, three feet
away from where Dad guards
each day in his hand-carved chair.
There's no reason for him to stand up
and answer its call, her friends
the only ones who phone, eager
to hear the day's vice-by-vice report.
He smokes cigarette after cigarette,
free from the foundry's core room,
no longer able to pour molten steel
into railroad part molds. Head hung low,
he waits for fishing friends to come
and drive him to the creek,
bait, rods, and reels left home.

## Hide

I remember watching Dad put chains on
our Rambler's tires in winter. Come spring, he
would take them off, hang them in the cow barn
for when he'd need to beat the living cow's
hides. He'd give them a lash when Babci cried
for her oldest son, now dead; another
when Mother wore her dry-clean-only dress
to visit the minister on Mondays;
again when letters arrived from my half-
sister—stories of bruises her husband gave her;
and then when Mother decided
I was too old, at five, to hear Dad's songs
seated on his lap.

                   I don't remember
seeing broken skin on those cows. I do
remember stroking their faces as they chewed,
how the field grass tickled me. I don't
remember them or Dad being taken away
after the chains broke, forced into
the backs of vehicles by coveralled men,
all complaints ignored. Could the cow's hides
have been the leather he stitched between

sedatives and shock therapy, crafted into belts
that later hung unused in the closet?
I remember the day he came home, how
he endlessly traced the grain of his new wallet
and asked with absent-minded eyes

*Do you know me?*

*spattered*

grease on the kitchen floor

a small man
in undershirt and jockeys

a woman's
beehived head abuzz

words
threaten fluorescent air

a bread knife
becomes a sword

a teen
wields a cast-iron pan

a girl
dreams of horses

tails
swish away persistent flies

*That Year*

He didn't hunt that year, spent
instead the hastened autumn baking
apple pies. Red Delicious he liked to eat
raw—too sweet for pie—cored,
peeled, then sliced by the same precise
hand that had carved the handle on the
knife he always used.

        Dad's pies earned no
medals, no *hmms* followed by sighs
of satisfaction. Still, he baked. Every
few days another emerged from the oven
while hunting buddies donned
handwarmers and camo, carried rifles
into woods following deer sign
in snow.

        From the kitchen window, Dad
watched flakes tumble as he over-floured
another crust rolled out too thick, wanting
a solid foundation for his filling. To the apples
he added twice the sugar and half the cinnamon
the recipe required, buried them in their doughy

coffin and baked them in the time it took
to smoke ten cigarettes.

> An eight-point buck fell with one shot,
> an easy weight for three men. Al
> gutted the deer before loading it
> into his pick-up and rejoined
> the others in their venison quest.

Twelve cigarettes
after turning the oven off, Dad cut
into the pie—halves, quarters, eighths—
and served us both, the filling still warm.

## February

Bad weather, like
two weeks in 1979
when Buffalo
would have been glad
for zero. The same
two weeks you
lingered over your
body, watching it
give up on you.
Were you angry
I did not keep
my promise?
That at nineteen
I did not know
how to bring you back
from the sanctuary
no one could
reach? Now I know
that place well.
I cannot hear you
singing here so
I travel there often,
through the multiverse,

hoping to find myself
age three again,
waiting for you
to wake me in my crib.

## Appendage

He chewed his thumb nail to its pith;
the same thumb flicked away her tears
when her two-wheeler dumped her into petals
and thorns, the thumb that held the hot
needle to her own to remove a rooted sliver,
the thumb that closed his grip on her hand
as she stepped onto the fresh ivory runner
the day he gave her to another, the thumb
that massaged her infant daughter's gums
until that first gleam of white bore through.

## Saved

Before the days of garbage men,
Dad burned our trash in a pile
clear of the woods
where pheasants hid
and watched orange waves
transform headlines, obits, weddings,
and births into ash curls that rose
then wafted in the chill
before falling back
for a second incineration.
An occasional can
found its way to the burn pile
where flames would tongue
its edges in futile effort—
consuming only the label—
contents spent elsewhere.
As Dad poked the refuse
attempting to escape,
I wondered how many
personalities had ended there
in vaporized latex
and why I was not among them.

*Alive*

I remember a summer afternoon
from my youth, five teen girls
swimming in a quarry, eating
happenstance sandwiches in bikinis.
As I looked at Mother's motionless chest,
I remembered that day and driving home,
our bras flapping like flags
around the car's antenna, our breasts
floating free beneath our shirts.

## About the Author

Claudia M. Stanek grew up in the blur of murmurs and silences of English while living on the border of Polish-Catholic steel town Depew and German-Lutheran rural Lancaster in Western New York state. She received her MFA from Bennington College (2007). She is a founding member of non-profit Just Poets in Rochester, NY. Her work has appeared in *Conte Online*, *Redactions: Poetry, Poetics & Prose*, *Euphony*, *Fourth River*, and *Roanoke Review*, among others, as well as the anthologies *Cinquainicity* (Palettes & Quills, 2009), *Community Voices* (University of Rochester, 2009), *Knocking on the Silence: A Finger Lakes Anthology* (Foothills, 2005), *Le Mot Juste* (Foothills, 2005-2010), and *Common Intuitions* (Palettes & Quills, 2003). Her poem "Housewife" was selected by composer Judith Lang Zaimont as the inspiration for a commissioned libretto for the 2009 Eastman School of Music's Women in Music Festival. Claudia received a Significant Opportunity Stipend from the Arts & Cultural Council of Greater Rochester as well as a writer's residency in Bialystok, Poland. Her work has been translated into as well as published in Polish. She lives in East Rochester, NY where she and her rescued pets enjoy viewing the birches from her morning reading nook.

## About the Book

*Language You Refuse to Learn* was designed by Bertha Rogers. The typeface for the cover is Adobe InDesign CS6 Gentium Book Type and Venetian 301 Book Type for the text. The type was selected and set by Kyrra Howard and proofread by Lawrence E. Shaw. The book was printed on 60-lb., acid-free, recycled paper in the United States of America. This first edition is limited to copies in paper wrappers.

## About Bright Hill Press

OUR MISSION: To seek out, study, and collect the work of early and contemporary writers, storytellers, and artists, and to publish, disseminate, and present that work through publications and educational and public programs for the larger community.

OUR HISTORY: Bright Hill Press/Word Thursdays was founded in 1992 by Bertha Rogers, with the assistance of Ernest M. Fishman. A writer, teacher, and visual artist, Ms. Rogers serves as the organization's executive director and editor in chief. Mr. Fishman has served BHP as president and/or chief financial officer since its beginnings. Bright Hill Press is located at Bright Hill Literary Center, 94 Church Street, in the hamlet of Treadwell, in New York's Catskill Mountain Region; program participants are from Delaware, Otsego, Sullivan, Schoharie, Broome, and Chenango counties as well. Programs and services have grown to meet the stated and implied needs of both youth and adult populations in those counties, as well as the needs of the literary community in New York State and beyond. BHP's current administrative focus is on long-range planning, in order to better fulfill its mission and expand its programs.

OUR ARTISTIC PHILOSOPHY: Bright Hill Press is dedicated to increasing audiences' appreciation of the writing arts and oral traditions that comprise American literature, and to encouraging and furthering the tradition of oral poetry and writing in the Catskills. Writers and artists who participate in BHP's programs are selected for their artistic excellence, their ability and willingness to work within a community setting, and the diversity of their backgrounds, genres, and styles. BHP understands that recognition of the need for a literary community and a commitment to lifelong learning are critical aspects of audience development; the organization's programs for children and adults engender the spirit, craft, and imagination that make this possible.

OUR PROGRAMS are offered to people of all ages. Current program offerings include:

- Word Thursdays, a reading series begun in 1992 and presenting open readings followed by readings and discussion by featured authors;
- Bright Hill Books, publishing anthologies as well as poetry collections and chapbooks and interdisciplinary collections by individual authors since 1994;
- Bright Hill Library & Internet Wing, since 2004, a facility with more than 10,000 titles of prose and poetry, art, reference, nature, and children's books for the immediate and larger community;
- New York State's Literary Web Site, nyslittree.org (since 1999), and the New York State Literary Map (in print and online), developed and administered by BHP, in partnership with the New York State Council on the Arts;
- Word Thursdays Share the Words HS Poetry Mentoring Program and Competition, affording young poets a chance to write and present their own poetry in a public competition since 1996;
- Word Thursdays Literary Workshops for Kids & Adults, offering, since 1994, innovative programs that celebrate and incorporate the elegant use of words with other disciplines;
- Word & Image Gallery, dedicated, since 2002, to presenting works by regional and national artists that integrate words and images;
- Patterns, BHLC's Literary Garden/Park for the whole community, landscaped and created by Catskill Outdoor Educational Corps, a program of Americorps at SUNY Delhi;
- BHLC Internship Program for College and HS Students, offering, since 1994, students an opportunity to learn the business of literature.

GOVERNANCE: Bright Hill Press/Word Thursdays is an independent 501 (c) (3), not-for-profit corporation governed by a board of directors representing the community the organization serves, and an advisory board from the larger community.

## Bright Hill Press
## At Hand Poetry Chapbook Award Series

*Language You Refuse to Learn*  Claudia M. Stanek  2014  $10
(2013 Poetry Chapbook Award Co-Winner, Selected by Martin Mitchell)

*The Cards We've Drawn*  Scot Slaby  2014  $10
(2013 Poetry Chapbook Award Co-Winner, Selected by Martin Mitchell)

*Self-Portrait / Sixteen Sevenlings*  Rodger Moody  2013  $10
(2012 Poetry Chapbook Award)

*A Tide of A Hundred Mountains*  Richard Levine  2012  $10
(2011 Poetry Chapbook Award)

*Counterpoint*  Jean Hollander  2011  $10
(2010 Poetry Chapbook Award)

*The Infatuations and Infidelities of Pronouns*
Christopher Bursk  2011  $10
(2009 Poetry Chapbook Award)

*Haywire*  Rachel Contreni Flynn  2009  $10
(2007 Poetry Chapbook Award)

*The Cut Worm*  Douglas Korb  2008  $8
(2006 Poetry Chapbook Award)

*A Sense of Place*  Bhikshuni Weisbrot  2007  $8
(2005 Poetry Chapbook Award)

*Gobbo: A Solitaire's Opera*  David Cappella  2006  $8
(2004 Poetry Chapbook Award)

*Web-Watching*  Bruce Bennett  2005  $8
(2003 Poetry Chapbook Award)

*Possum*  Shelby Stephenson  2004  $8
(2002 Poetry Chapbook Award)

*First Probe to Antarctica*  Barry Ballard  2003  $8
(2001 Poetry Chapbook Award)

*Inspiration Point*  Matthew J. Spireng  2002  $8
(2000 Poetry Chapbook Award)

*What Falls Away*  Steve Lautermilch  2001  $8
(1999 Poetry Chapbook Award)

*Whatever Was Ripe*  William Jolliff  1999  $8
(1997 Poetry Chapbook Award)

*The Man Who Went Out for Cigarettes*
Adrian Blevins 1996  $8  (1995 Poetry Chapbook Award)


## Bright Hill Press At Hand
## Fiction Chapbook Award Series

*Low Country Stories*  Lisa Harris  $8
(1996 Fiction Chapbook Award)

*Boxes*  Lisa Harris  $8
(1998 Fiction Chapbook Award)

## Bright Hill Press At Hand
## Poetry Chapbook Series

*In the Garden*   Susan Fantl Spivack   2013   $10

*Dancing Bears*   Karen Fabiane   2011   $10

*A Plastic Bag of Red Cells*   Annie Petrie-Sauter   2010   $10

*Skunk Night Sonnets*   Daniel Waters   2009   $10

*The Wooden Bowl*   Sharon Ruetenik   2009   $10

*Love in the End*   Mary Kay Rummel   2008   $10

*Effects of Sunlight in the Fog*   Alan Catlin   2008   $10

*Picking Up*   Evelyn Duncan   2008   $8

*The Lily Poems*   Liz Rosenberg   2008   $8

*The Courtship and Other Tales*   Kathryn Ugoretz   2007   $8

*Hairpin Loop*   Anne Blonstein   2007   $8

*The Coriolis Effect*   Michael Dowdy   2007   $8

*It Does Not*   Julia Suarez   2006   $8

*In Late Fields*   Steven Ostrowski   2006   $8

*Instinct*   Joanna Straughn   2006   $8

*Autobiography of My Hand*   Kurt S. Olsson   2006   $8

*Degrees of Freedom*   Nicholas Johnson   2006   $8

*Walking Back the Cat*   Lynn Pattison   2005   $8

*The Spirit of the Walrus*   ElisaVietta Ritchie   2005   $8

*LightsOut*   Tom Lavazzi   2005   $8

*The Last Best Motif*   Naton Leslie   2005   $6

## Bright Hill Press
## Poetry Book Award Series

*Tonight's Quiet*   Constance Norgren   2014   $16
(2012 Poetry Book Award) Chosen by Alfred Corn

*What I Can Tell You*   Ruth Moon Kempher   2013   $16
(2011 Poetry Book Award) Chosen by Philip Mosley

*Outside Come In*   Ryan J. Browne   2012   $16
(2010 Poetry Book Award) Chosen by Neil Shepard

*Almond Town*   Margaret Young   2011   $16
(2009 Poetry Book Award) Chosen by Colette Inez

*Raven's Paradise*   Red Hawk   2010   $16
(2008 Poetry Book Award) Chosen by Rhina Espaillat

*Infinite Beginnings*   Lucyna Prostko   2009   $16
(2007 Poetry Book Award) Chosen by Joan Larkin

*How the Brain Grew Back Its Own History*  Liz Beasley  2008  $14
  (2006 Poetry Book Award) Chosen by Jay Rogoff

*Need-Fire*  Becky Gould Gibson  2007  $14
(2005 Poetry Book Award) Chosen by Liz Rosenberg

*The Artist As Alice: From a Photographer's Life*
Darcy Cummings  2006  $14
(2004 Poetry Book Award) Chosen by Carolyne Wright

*The Aerialist*  Victoria Hallerman  2005  $12
(2003 Poetry Book Award)  Chosen by Martin Mitchell

*Strange Gravity*  Lisa Rhoades  2004  $12
(2002 Poetry Book Award) Chosen by Elaine Terranova

*The Singer's Temple*  Barbara Hurd  2003  $12
(2001 Poetry Book Award) Chosen by Richard Frost

*Heart, with Piano Wire*  Richard Deutch  2002  $12
(2000 Poetry Book Award) Chosen by Maurice Kenny

*My Father & Miro & Other Poems*  Claudia M. Reder  2001  $12
  (1999 Poetry Book Award) Chosen by Colette Inez

*Traveling Through Glass*  Beth Copeland Vargo  2000  $12
(1998 Poetry Book Award) Chosen by Karen Swenson

*To Fit Your Heart into the Body*  Judith Neeld  1999  $12
(1997 Poetry Book Award) Chosen by Richard Foerster

*Blue Wolves*  Regina O'Melveny  1997  $12
(1996 Poetry Book Award) Chosen by Michael Waters

---

*My Own Hundred Doors*   Pam Bernard  1996   $10
(1995 Poetry Book Award) Chosen by Carol Frost


## Bright Hill Press Poetry Book Series

*Orenoque, Wetumka*   Robert Bensen   2012   $18

*Every Infant's Blood*   Graham Duncan  2002   $14.95

*Flares and Fathoms*   Margot Farrington  2005   $14


## Bright Hill Press Anthologies

*Speaking the Words Anthology*  1994   $6.95

*The Word Thursdays Anthology of Poetry & Fiction*  1995  $12.95

*The Second Word Thursdays Anthology:*
*Poetry & Prose by Bright Hill Press Writers*  1999  $19.95


## Bright Hill Press Word & Image Series

*Suddenly There Were Leaves Anthology*  2013
*Poetry & Prose by Main View Gallery & Studio Artists*
Edited by Bertha Rogers

*Breathing the Monster Alive*   Eric Gansworth  2006   $16

*On the Watershed: The Natural World of New York's*
*Catskill Mountain Region/ Catskill Student Writers*
Edited by Bertha Rogers  2001    $14.95

*Out of the Catskills & Just Beyond*
*Literary & Visual Works by Catskill Writers & Artists*
Edited by Bertha Rogers  1997    $24

*Iroquois Voices, Iroquois Visions*
*A Celebration of Contemporary Six Nations Arts*
Edited by Bertha Rogers,  with Maurice Kenny,
Tom Huff, & Robert Bensen  1996    $15

## Bright Hill Press Exhibition Series

*Bright Hill Book Arts* 2010    $16
Edited by Bertha Rogers
Curated by Elsi Vassdal Ellis & Bertha Rogers

*Bright Hill Book Arts* 2008    $16
Edited by Bertha Rogers
Juried by Keith Smith & Bertha Rogers

*Bright Hill Book Arts* 2007    $16
Edited by Bertha Rogers
With commentary by Karen Hanmer & Bertha Rogers

*Bright Hill Book Arts* 2006    $16
Edited by Bertha Rogers
With commentary by Richard Minksy & Bertha Rogers

*Bright Hill Book Arts 2005*   $16
Edited by Bertha Rogers
With commentary by Edward Hutchins & Bertha Rogers

*Bright Hill Book Arts 2004*   $12
Edited by Bertha Rogers
With commentary by Nancy Callahan & Louise Neaderland

*Bright Hill Book Arts 2003*   $10
Edited by Bertha Rogers
With  commentary by Rory Golden & Keith Smith

*Bright Hill Book Arts 2002*   $10
Edited by Bertha Rogers
With commentary by Richard Minsky & Peter Verheyen

# Ordering Bright Hill Press Books

BOOKSTORES & INDIVIDUALS: Bright Hill Press books are distributed to the trade and to the public by Small Press Distribution (spd@spdbooks.org), 1341 Seventh St., Berkeley, CA 94710-1409; Baker & Taylor (800-775-1500), 1120 Route 22 East, Bridgewater, NJ 08807; and North Country Books (regional titles), 311 Turner St., POB 217, Utica, NY 13501-1727. Our books may also be found at BN.com, Amazon.com, at your local bookstores, and at Bright Hill Press's website, brighthillpress.org (payment may be made by credit card or through PayPal). If your local bookstores do not stock Bright Hill Press books, please ask them to special order, or write to us at Bright Hill Press, 94 Church Street, Treadwell, NY 13846-4607 or to our e-mail address: wordthur@stny.rr.com, or call at 607-829-5055. Further information may be found on our website: brighthillpress.org; or by calling 607-829-5055.